Narco-State

Cesar Kenny Pérez Rojas

Narco-State

Ediciones "CK"
Cochabamba - Bolivia
2019

Title of the work:
Narco Estado

Autor:
Cesar Kenny Pérez Rojas

References:
Email: kennyperezrojas@gmail.com
Mobil phone - WhatsApp: 76961967

Facebook:
#kennypérezr

Text review and design:
Cesar Kenny Perez Rojas

Editing data:
Editions "CK".
Special limited edition.
June 2019

Printed in:
"CK Craft Workshops"

Cochabamba-Bolivia.

Source :https://ssociologos.com/2019/03/03/el-peru-es-un-narcoestado/

INTRODUCTION

Within a state, the political regime, the public institutions, politicians, the police, the army, lose credibility and thus the legitimacy they should have because of the development of drug trafficking; drug trafficking can compete and surpass the sovereignty of the state. The formation of a Narco-State is a threat to the national security and socio-political stability of any country. Drug trafficking has relevance as a social phenomenon, it influences all aspects of society, in the economic, political, cultural and international context.

This short research paper discusses how this business develops, how it unfolds. This text took as reference the States in which drug trafficking has developed rampantly, such as Mexico, Colombia and Bolivia. It looks at what drug trafficking is in politics, what is organized crime, how drug trafficking influences the culture, and the economic power that this industry obtains, economic power that is used for political purposes, going so far as to corrupt the different authorities of the state and it's institutions.

Narco-State is a term that is intimately linked to the concepts of drug trafficking, money laundering, terrorism, white trafficking, prostitution, corruption and many ills that have been generated in recent decades, thanks to the presence of the international mafia and the so-called drug cartels.

1.- STATE

1.1.- Concepts and definitions

A State consists of territory, sovereignty over that territory, government and population, is constantly evolving, it is a society, a political community; the state is a political organization, it is a political reality that aims to seek the common good of society. It was Nicholas Machiavelli the father of political science who introduced the State with a legal -political character in his work "The Prince", "*All States, all the dominations that have exercised and exercise sovereignty over men, have been and are republics or principalities*"[1]. in this text the author proposed that the ruler of a state should devote himself fully to what the art of governing is, in order to avoid the decline of the State and strengthen it; for this thinker the power that a ruler acquires and sustains, translates into the strengthening of the state.

For the political philosopher Thomas Hobbes man is always in constant war with his fellowmen, there is mutual distrust among men, they are always in a state of continuous enmity, a situation of all against all, that is why the state arises; it is established as a pact of mutual trust,

---

[1] Machiavelli Nicholas, 1999 , p. 6 .

the State as a common power to keep everyone at bay, the state as a coercive power.

"The generation of a state. The only way to build such common power, capable of defending them against the invasion of foreigners and against the insults of others, assuring them in such a way that by their own activity and by the fruits of the earth they can nourish themselves and live satisfied , is to confer all his power and strength on a man or to an assembly of men, all of whom, by plurality of vows, can reduce their wills to a will. This is tantamount to saying: choosing a man or an assembly of men who represents his personality, and that each considers himself as his own and is also recognized as the author of anything that does or promotes who represents his person, in those things that concern the common peace and security; who, moreover, submit their wills to the will of him, and his judgments in his view. This is more than just consent or harmony; is a real unity of all this in one and the same person, instituted by every man's covenant with others, in such a way as if each one said to everyone: I authorize and transfer to this man or assembly of men my right to rule myself , on the condition that you transfer your right to him, and authorize all his acts in the same way. Once this is done the multitude thus united in a person is called STATE, in Latin, CIVITAS. This is the generation of that great LEVIATAN, or rather

(speaking with more reverence), of that mortal god, to whom we must, under the immortal God, our peace and our defense."[2]

Likewise, among the functions of the State are: providing economic, social and political order, establishing peace, justice, well-being and security; *"The mission of a state is to keep the people at peace, within, and to defend them from foreign invasion"*.[3]

For the thinker John Jacob Rousseau, the state aims to protect the common interest of all, says that humans must be governed by a legitimate administration, a political community that is based on the convention between men, a collective pact, an act of association called "Social Contract", the whole of the society subject to the general will, thus constituting the State. *"The public person thus constituted, by the union of all others, once took the name of city and today that of republic or political body, which is called the State."*[4]

Likewise, for the German sociologist Max Weber, one of the founders of modern social theory and scholar of political theory, the State is

---

[2] HOBBES Thomas, pp. 71-72.
[3] HOBBES Thomas, p.106.
[4] ROUSSEAU Juan Jacob, 1999, pp. 15-16.

that collective that has the legitimate monopoly of the use of force, for him the state is, "*that human community that within a certain territory (the "territory" is a distinctive element), claims (successfully) for itself the monopoly of legitimate physical violence*".[5] For this author, the State is a relationship of dominance between individuals, which is based on legitimate violence, "The State, *like all associations or political entities that have historically preceded it, is a relationship of domination of men over men, supported by legitimate violence.*"[6] According to this sociologist, the exclusive use of this force would allow to resolve the conflicts of coexistence and sociability, the coercion administered legally.

1.2.- Modern State

To describe the development of the State, it can be said that it came with the rebirth of new ideas that emerged regarding the political organization of society; the modern state is established and one of the most important features of it is the consolidation and institutionalization of a legitimate authority.

---

[5] WEBER Max, p. 2.

[6] Ibídem, 3.

"The modern state is an association of institutional domination that has successfully sought to monopolize within a territory legitimate physical violence as a means of domination and which in order to achieve this purpose has brought together all the material means in the hands of its leader and has expropriated all officials who previously had them in their own right, replacing them with their own supreme hierarchies."[7]

1.3.- Rule of law

Another condition presented by the State is the rule of law, the rule of law is in force when a State is governed by legal norms, legal precepts, there is a political constitution, there are laws and the individuals are subject to them. According to Roberto Ruiz Diaz Labrano author of "The Rule of Law some elements and conditions for its effective validity" the rule of law *"is the product of a long evolution, in which the principles that today contribute to establish their most significant contours, such as the subjection of rulers to the law and respect for the division of powers."*[8]

---

[7] Ibídem, 6.
[8] RUIZ Roberto, p. 2

In a Narco-State, while there is a scenario in which the rule of law is in force, corruption stands out, especially for state institutions, institutions that have the aim of maintaining and strengthening the rule of law, these are corrupted by drug trafficking, they get perverted.

1.4.- Coup

Likewise, in a state often happens what is the coup d'éature, it occurs when a group of society through violent and surprising action, decides to take power by force, to assume the government of a state illegally, illegitimately and irregularly, going against the rule of law.

The causes of a coup can be many, including social and political crises; there are also political figures, ambitious and daring who organize and encourage coups and then take power, they use conspiracy, different strategies and political tactics; usurp power through surprise actions to govern and dominate citizens. As soon as a new government is established in this way, reforms are made and different policies are implemented to exercise control and appease the population, such as the dissemination of political propaganda to give legitimacy to the new government.

1.5.- Political propaganda

In a state exists political propaganda, an activity responsible for spreading the dominant ideology, a legitimate state is composed of a government that exercises control over the ideologies and the way of thinking of their inhabitants; there must be an efficient propaganda apparatus, which appeases the citizens so that there is no dissent; this indoctrination has to be inherent in the formation of the citizen of the State, it can be in the education system and it has to be applied efficiently.

You must have the population controlled, that means having the control of ideologies, general culture, religions and information; North Korea can be mentioned as a country with a controlled society, it is isolated from the world. Generally ideological control manifests itself in states, where there are dictatorial governments run by a single party, as soon as it appears any type of movement or subversive tendency, it is detected, pursued and suppressed using entities that are engaged in this task, such as the police, political police or secret police; these are bodies dedicated to maintaining political and social stability within a state. Identity, traditions, symbols, religion, language are some elements that must be preserved in a society for stability and cultural continuity, just as political institutions may be maintained; political legitimacy must always be established and disseminated throughout society.

1.6.- Supra-State Entities

There is what is called Suprastatal Entities, these are those entities that are established for collaboration between states, so that they can relate and coordinate policies that suit the whole, this entities have power and influence over their members E.g. the (UN), the OAS (Organization of American States), the EU (European Union) are supra-state organizations. States tend to partner in supra-state organizations to determine actions and policies for the whole, they are grouped together to meet the demands of the global economy, international markets, etc. as is the case with OPEC (Organization of Petroleum Exporting Countries).

The power and influence of these organizations can outweigh the power of a single state, turning them into regulating organizations.

The Member States of supra-state organizations have common purposes, they partner to better organize themselves, so that they can achieve their common goals.

1.7.- International influence

International influence towards a state is always in force; in some states such as North Korea and Cuba, communist countries with an impressive propaganda apparatus, the ideas are imposed on the population and they brainwash the individuals; international influence on the population of this countries cannot be tolerated or allowed, the culture and influence of other countries can change people, as to who they are and what they would like.

the outside world influences on the ideology of the community, changing the thinking on many issues among them political issues, that's what the authorities don't want, freedom of expression, certain information, knowledge, the media, the culture of other countries, music and television programs are prohibited and limited in these countries, as they can become destabilizing elements for a state.

The Sociopolitical phenomena called globalization, because of the economic, social and cultural demands, tend to transform states, it happened in China, a country that was forced to make reforms because of the influence of this Phenomenon.

1.8.- The weakness of the State

Another characteristic of the State is its weakness, the weakness of the State manifests itself when within it, socio-political forces emerge, forces that have the capacity to challenge the authority of the state with respect to political hegemony within the State; this scenario is in force in Colombia where the Colombian government shares power with guerrilla and drug trafficking groups, dividing and weakening the state.

"Large remote and isolated territories are opened to illicit drugs outside the networks and principles of political legitimacy of the State and disconnected from the national road network, but interconnected by "unknown" rivers in state mapping. These territories, many located on international borders, can be transformed into ideal niches for

guerrillas, traditional smuggling or cultivation, chemical processing and air transport of illicit drugs." [9]

1.9.- State policies

Among the essential elements of a State are its policies, state policies, these are those fundamental, important and strategic policies of the State, they can be of military nature, in the same way they can refer to national security or some vindication; state policies differ from government policies in that they are permanent policies. State policies relate to matters that fall within the entire society of a country, which means the national interest and the validity of these must be permanent, in some cases of a perpetual nature regardless of those in the Government, for example. Bolivia has a state policy on maritime issues with Chile.

Therefore, the State in this text is understood as a political institution, a community with a political regime and legal organization, with institutions that regulate society, holds a coercive power and is constantly evolving; the State is a

---

[9] PALACIOS Marco y SERRANO Monica, p. 122.

political reality that aims at the common good of society, being it´s most relevant components: the society, the territory, the population and the government; the State is the place where social and political order is established.

2. DRUG TRAFFICKING

2.1.- Concept

"A concept that integrates the neologism narco-state is drug trafficking (narco), drug trafficking is an illegal industry worldwide, consisting in the production, distribution, sale and transport of narcotics, it's the illicit trade of narcotics; according to the author of the essay: "The Evolution of Drug Trafficking in Mexico" Oscar Contreras, drug trafficking can be defined as *"the trafficking of illegal drugs that are smuggled from one place to another".*[10]

2.2.- Characteristics

The characteristics of drug trafficking are:

1) Drug Sales
2) Market Control
3) Drug Consumption and Recycling
4) Substance cultivation
5) Drug Manufacturing
6) Drug Distribution
7) Drug Transport

---

[10] CONTRERAS VELASCO Oscar, (s.f.), pág. 1.

In jurisdictions where there is legislation prohibiting the use and sale of drugs, an illegal market is created. According to Jorge Chabat, drug trafficking has the following characteristics:

"It is a global phenomenon, however, it does not affect all States equally. b) It is a consensual crime in which both the victim and the offender agree. c) There is no clear criterion of success in it's combat. d) Figures on production and profits are unreliable. (e) It is a crime created about a century ago by a decision of the community of states to declare some drugs illegal. f) It is difficult to establish a line that separates the unwillingness of a state's in its combat from a lack of capacity (g) It has an unprecedented capacity of

accumulation, because of the large amounts of money it generates in very short periods of time."[11]

2.3.- Origin and evolution

To describe the origin and progress of this industry, it can be said that the drug trade already existed in the nineteenth century in China, where opium smoking was common and it was the English that provided this narcotic to the Asian country; since then people that engaged in drug trafficking have been able to adapt to different social contexts and have developed themselves to be more efficient, including elements such as organization and innovation in their business; according to Lilian Paola Ovalle Marroquín the author of "Drug trafficking and power. A field of struggle for legitimacy", the evolution of these criminal groups ocurres as follows:

"The persistence of these networks and their strategies to circumvent legal obstacles for their development, shows their capacity for innovation, competitiveness and adaptability. This fact is especially observable in the transformation of these groups, in which, from rustic organizations, have become

---

[11] CHABAT George, Sept. 2005, p. 3.

specialized networks with a planned division of labor".[12]

One of the first treaties to be signed with regard to drug regulation is the International Convention on restriction on the use and trafficking of Opium, Morphine, Cocaine and its salts, signed in The Hague on January 23 1912. The drug-trafficking boom began roughly in the 1960s, first with the marketing of marijuana, then to cocaine and other drugs; In addition, the countries of South America began to have prominence internationally for their coca leaf crops.

2.4.- Drug trafficking, power and society

The economic power and political influence obtained by drug traffickers allows them to have the ability to replace the state in many aspects, citing Ovalle Marroquín:

"The narcos have come to play the role of the state and have responded to the demands of communities in housing, public space, education, recreation, among others. In this way, they have been

---

[12] OVALLE MARROQUIN Lilian Paola, March 2010, p. 91.

able to crystallize a legitimacy discourse of their actions, by presenting themselves socially as 'people committed to regional development".[13]

The drug traffickers by achieving a degree of legitimacy before society, manage to challenge the authority of the government, they become a danger to the governance and political stability of states; it is through the perversion, corrupting and intimidation of the authorities that they are attaining this goal. A report by the United Nations Office on Drugs and Crime, called THE THREAT OF DRUG TRAFFIKING IN AMERICA, describes this phenomenon as follows: "Traffickers pose a direct threat to governance, fueling corruption and even threatening or killing high-level public employees who oppose them."[14]

Drug trafficking gains its power from the money it produces, that money allows the corrupting of government authorities and different public figures, increasing their power and

---

[13] Ibídem, 85.
[14] NACIONES UNIDAS, Octubre 2008, pág. 39.

influence; the power of drug trafficking increases when it engages with different armed groups, subversive groups, guerrillas, groups that go against the established order, thus making this business a political instrument. At the international level, this business involves many States, from the cultivation of the narcotic substances, obtaining the raw material, refining and transferring them, etc. Countries are forced to work together to develop different strategies to combat this industry; according to the United Nations:

"Drug traffickers do not respect borders, and the only way to combat them is through cross-border cooperation. Although unilateral or bilateral approaches can address parts of the problem, only a multilateral approach can deal with the issue as a whole."[15]

The states through their governments implement different policies to combat drug trafficking, depending on how developed the business is in the country, whether there is some tolerance and acceptance in society, or whether

---

[15] Ídem.

there is a permanent and open war against drugs. International pressure, the degree in which public institutions are susceptible to corruption and government credibility, should be considered when applying a policy; these elements influence a country's international relations and the efficiency of the fight against drugs. The production and trafficking of narcotics is constantly evolving, and influences various states by the economic power obtained; according to the sociologist John Jairo Aristizabal, referring to the Colombian context, states that *"drug trafficking is a destabilizing element for the entire democratic society, generating huge sums of money for armed groups outside the law"*.[16]

From an economic point of view, drug trafficking is very profitable, generating astronomical gains, for this and other reasons it is a business that is constantly growing and expanding; drug trafficking influences various social scenarios because of the economic power it gains. Similarly, this industry influences the economies of states by the huge amount of money it generates, profits are used to invest in other businesses and a lot of wealth is created, it

---

[16] ARISTIZABAL VILLADA John Jairo, 2006, p. 51.

also serves to gain political influence through the corruption of authorities and the financing of political parties; criminal organizations engaged in this business are such as family clans, cartels, syndicates, guerrillas, paramilitaries, etc. This organizations use the profits made to consolidate and grow their power and influence; the money that is produced becomes power.

People engaged in drug trafficking risk being killed or entering prison, the decision to enter this business is a decision of life and death, imprisonment and freedom; many of the people in this industry argue that they do so out of necessity, because of the lack of employment opportunities, and to emerge in society. Addicts are the ones who keep this business going and the profits generated are astronomical; the value that the drug acquires depends on where it is marketed.

Drug traffickers are organized in different ways, the market and the territory where they operate is dived among them, industrial methods are used for the production of drugs which allows to produce a narcotic on a large scale, generating great profits; drug trafficking is seen as a way out of poverty and a way to gain power. With the globalization, the markets open up and people have more opportunities to sell drugs.

2.5.- Narco-Culture

The Narco-Culture arises in societies where drug trafficking has acquired a degree of legitimacy; there are heroes, art, music, movies, TV shows, clothing that represent what drug trafficking is, there are even saints. *"narco culture are those social manifestations that revolve around the world of narcotics trafficking."*[17]

The followers of drug-culture are not always people who are engaged in drug trafficking, they are people who like everything related to drug trafficking; in some countries drug traffickers are glorified and exalted, they are considered heroes and saints, as is the happened in Colombia with Pablo Escobar; stereotypes are formed as for example. linking Bolivia and Colombia to drug trafficking in the films, this are manifestations of a subculture.

---

[17] ALMADA Marcos, 07 / 2005, p. 1.

The TV series "Pablo Escobar, the Boss of Evil"

Source: https://www.amazon.ca/Pablo-Escobar-Patron-Del-Part/dp/B00BZC00Z2

Jesus Malverde, "the saint of the narcos", the business becomes art, the TV shows immerse themselves in the world of drugs and the music (narcocorridos) is to the traffickers.

Source: https://www.excelsior.com.mx/expresiones/2015/05/05/102253

There are those who make a lot of money from narco-culture and plan to keep doing it, among these are the clothing manufacturers, they design garments with the image of famous drug dealers, so are television productions like the series that refers to the life of Colombian drug trafficker Pablo Escobar, called "The Boss of Evil" thus turning a drug dealer into a cultural icon. Some drug traffickers help their communities by building churches, soccer fields, schools, building roads, etc. that's why their communities admire them and become local heroes. Greatness, generosity, power and violence are exalted, when children are asked what they want to be when they grow up many say drug traffickers, drug-culture results in the tolerance and acceptance of drug trafficking on the part of the society, who believe in certain degree that it's not bad to be a drug dealer.

2.6.- Influence of drug trafficking on politics

Drug trafficking influences politics, so that drug traffickers can influence politics they resort to methods such as intimidation, corruption, murder, etc. that allows drug traffickers to do business with impunity, they share their wealth with many public officials and political figures; it's the money that allows them to gain political influence, they gain that influence through the corruption of the authorities. Many times when the power of a state's government is overwhelmed by the power of drug trafficking, the state calls for the cooperation of other countries to fight against it, as is the case in Colombia that receives the help of the United States.

Drug trafficking shapes a state by the political power and economic power it has, criminal organizations buy weapons, finance politicians, associate and collaborate with armed groups, guerrilla groups, finance coups, finance terrorist attacks, threaten journalists, murder authorities, judges and political figures; they take over communities through corruption and intimidation, execute assassinations, create and finance paramilitary groups, etc. The leaders and politicians who are rising on the political stage are associated with drug trafficking to benefit themselves politically and when links are discovered between public authorities and drug traffickers, the matter becomes a scandal, what arises is called "narco-politics", this neologism is used to describe the intimate relationship that exists between politicians and drug trafficking.

"From the images of Pablo Escobar walking as an alternate congressman in Colombia, to the loss of the

visa of the then President of the same country, Ernesto Samper, because his campaign received millions of dollars from the so-called Cali Cartel, it is clear that the narco has always wanted to have politicians in their pocket. The best way is by the financing of the political campaigns".[18]

The drug traffickers finance bills, political campaigns, they threaten politicians, corrupt authorities to take care of their interests; once the drug traffickers are engaged in buying weapons and financing armed groups within a country, they become a powerful political force. It should also be noted that there has sometimes been a strategic partnership between a legitimate government and criminal organizations to confront a common enemy, as was the case with the partnership between the Government of Colombia and the Cali Cartel in its war against the Medellin Cartel; also some countries such as the United States use the drug trafficking as an argument to influence and intervene in other states, as happened in Panama that was invaded, this action led to the arrest of Manuel Noriega president of that country.

---

[18] SOBERON Ricardo, (18-7-2018).

2.7.- The fight against drug trafficking

With regard to the fight against drug trafficking, one may mention some of the strategies that society employs to combat this business, such as the collaboration between States and extradition treaties, especially with the United States; there are also specialized organizations dedicated to combating drug trafficking, such as the DEA (Drug Enforcement Agency) of the United States, FELCN (Special Drug Trafficking Force) of Bolivia. Proposals have emerged from some sectors of society, that suggest the regulation and legalization of drugs as a solution to the problem of substance abuse and drug trafficking; the issue of drug legalization is discussed more intensively, in states where the drug trafficking problem is rampant and has greater social relevance. Different policies and initiatives are applied, to combat drug trafficking, plans are created, the latest technology is used and different strategies are used to fight this industry.

According to internet information, books, documents, texts, videos and articles, these are some of the organizations worldwide that are engaged in drug trafficking, the Medellin Cartel, the Cali Cartel, cartel del Norte del Valle, Cartel de la Costa, Cartel of the suns, guerrillas and paramilitaries of Colombia, the Italian Mafia, the Italo-American Mafia, the Shower Posse of Jamaica, the street gangs in the United States, the gangs and criminal organizations that are in different prisons, the Velmelho Command of Brazil, the Sinaloa Cartel, Leyva Beltran Family Cartel, the Gulf Cartel, the Juarez Cartel, the Tijuana Cartel, the Mara Salvatrucha, the Pacific Cartel, the Felix Arellano Clan, the Michoacana Family, the Zetas, the Templar Knights, the Jalisco New Generation Cartel, the Acapulco Independent Cartel, the Japanese Yakuza, the Russian Mafia, the Chinese Mafia; on some occasions government agencies like the CIA (Central Intelligence Agency) of the United States where involved in drug trafficking, as a political-military strategy (Case Iran-Contra).

2.8.- Money laundering

Money laundering is:

The process through which the origin of funds generated through the exercise of some illegal or criminal activities is hidden (drug or narcotics trafficking, arms smuggling, corruption, fraud, prostitution, extortion, piracy and terrorism). The objective of the operation, which is usually carried out at various levels, is to make funds or assets obtained through illicit activities appear as the fruit of legitimate activities and flow smoothly into the financial system.[19]

Drug traffickers resort to what is called money laundering, to make use of the money generated from the sale of drugs, they need to launder it, make it legitimate, for that purpose they use banks, exchange houses and different businesses; people have to justify their income, their wealth, a person cannot simply generate a lot of money without being able to give an explanation of its provenance, especially if it comes from drug trafficking, this money is usually called dirty money, black money.

---

[19] Vicepresidencia de Supervisión de Procesos Preventivos Pág. 1

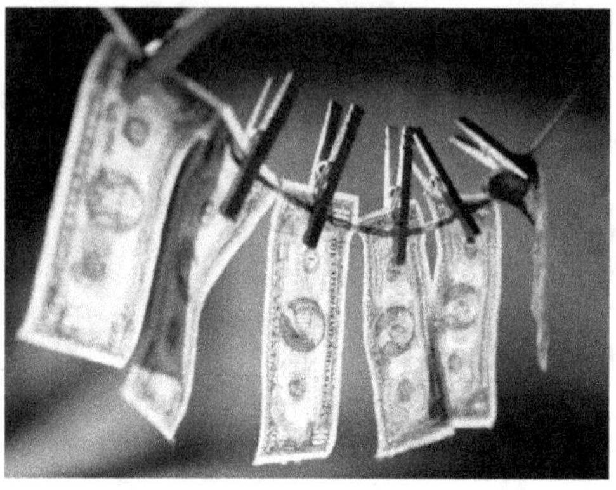

Source: https://www.dineroenimagen.com/economia/como-
funciona-el-lavado-de-dinero/87011

The 3 stages of money laundering:

1. **Placement**: This is the physical disposition of cash from criminal activities. During this initial phase, the money launderer introduces the illegal funds into the financial system and other businesses, both domestic and international.

2. **Stratification:** It is the separation of illicit funds from their source through a series of sophisticated financial transactions, the purpose is to blur the original transaction. This stage involves converting funds from illicit activities to another form and

creating complex financial transaction schemes to disguise the documented trail, the source and ownership of funds.

3. **Integration**: Is to give legitimate appearance to illicit wealth by re-entering it to the economy with commercial or personal transactions that appear to be normal. This phase involves placing laundered funds back into the economy to create a perception of legitimacy. The money launderer could choose to invest the funds in real estate, luxury goods or commercial projects, among others.[20]

2.9.- Narco-Terrorism

Narco-terrorism refers to terrorist actions committed by armed groups engaged in drug trafficking, like the activities of Colombia's Medellin Cartel, which exploded car bombs, killed policemen and exploded a commercial aircraft in mid-flight; likewise, narco-terrorism are the activities of subversive groups such as the FARC of Colombia (Revolutionary Armed Forces of Colombia), group that is engaged in the abduction of persons, they are also involved in drug-trafficking; it can be said that

---

[20] https://www.forbes.com.mx/las-3-etapas-del-lavado-de-dinero/

when guerrilla groups are associated with drug trafficking, arises what is called drug-guerrillas.

Flight 203 of Avianca, Colombia's main commercial airline; suffered a terrorist attack on the part of the Medellin Cartel, which was led by Pablo Escobar.

Source: https://www.infobae.com/america/colombia/2019/11/24/a-30-anos-del-dia-que-pablo-escobar-hizo-explotar-un-avion-comercial-y-mato-a-110-personas-pero-se-salvo-la-unica-a-la-que-queria-asesinar/

3.- PERSPECTIVES ABOUT THE NARCO-STATE

3.1.- Definitions

There are many definitions of different authors and social researchers, to what is a Narco-State, among them we can name that of the sociologist William Ortiz, who in his doctoral thesis called THE PARASTATES IN COLOMBIA, explains a situation in which drug trafficking achieves excessive power, having the ability to corrupt the authorities and challenge the authority of the Government, thus demonstrating institutional weakness, states that *"drug trafficking undoubtedly penetrates all social instances and is active in its various layers".*[21]

Ortiz describes a social context in which "the power of drug trafficking is of such magnitude that it changes and structures political forms when it deems it appropriate", this author conceives the Narco-State as a parallel state, a political community with a certain degree of autonomy in force within the country, a "parastate" that has as a fundamental pillar the drug trafficking business; for this sociologist, this

---

[21] ORTIZ JIMÉNEZ William, may 2006, p. 162.

industry for its power and influence acquires the characteristics of a state, *"drug trafficking is perhaps the parastate that most influences the Colombian state and political system".*[22]

Likewise, author Rubén Corona in his essay: "The narco, parallel state", referring to the country of Mexico, conceives the narco-State as a community in which drug trafficking, for its high degree of power and influence manages to become the de facto authority, turning it into a parallel state. *"_The rise of the narco as a "de facto" authority reveals that it is no exaggeration to start talking about a parallel narco state".*[23] According to Corona, the power that the drug traffickers manage to acquire, allows them to function as authorities. " *The power of these criminal gangs is enormous, and it is precisely what enables them to assert themselves as "men of government", capable of imposing on society a way of proceeding.*[24]

For Carolina Navarrete and Francisco Thoumi, authors of the document "Illegal Drugs and Human Rights of Peasants and Indigenous Communities: The Case of Bolivia", printed by the United Nations Educational, Scientific and

---

[22] Ibídem, 304.
[23] CORONA CADENA Rubén I. 2009, p. 220.
[24] Ibídem, 212.

Cultural Organization (UNESCO), the first Narco-State that was established in Latin America was the Bolivian in 1980, during the Government of The Gral. Luis García Meza, «*When General Luis García Meza rose to power through a coup in July 1980, the first "Narco-State" was established in Latin America* ».[25]

3.2.- Characteristic's

In a Narco-State the drug trafficking business works with impunity, there is a power structure that is responsible for protecting and promoting this activity, likewise, it is considered to be a Narco-State, a state where it the drug business is glorified, where people worships the drug traffickers and drugs; another feature of a Narco-State is the interdependence between political power and drug producers.

The main characteristics of a Narco-State are the following:

1) Corruption of Authorities
2) Organized Crime
3) Drug trafficking
4) Institutional weakness

---

[25] NAVARRETE FRIAS Carolina y THOUMI Francisco E., 2005, p. 20.

5) Money laundering

6) Narco-Culture

7) Violence

Different zones are formed within the State in which there is no authority, the authority is the drug traffickers who gain the acceptance of the communities with respect to their activities, by the projects they carry out in favor of the people, such as housing, schools, roads, sport fields, etc. projects that should be implemented by the Government and not by the drug traffickers, who function as autorithies.

Structure of a Narco-State

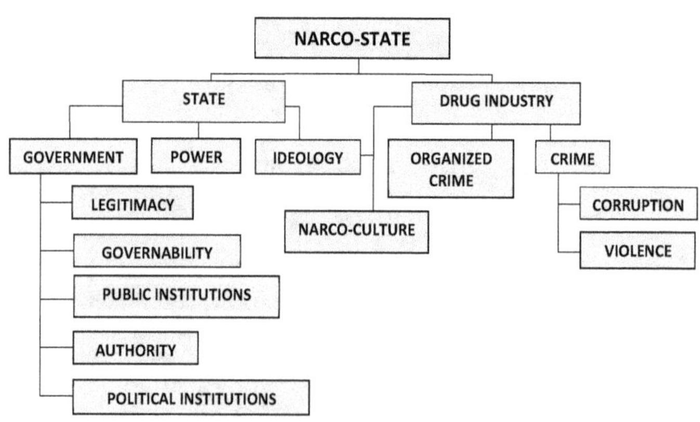

Source: PEREZ ROJAS, Cesar K. Degree thesis. 2018, p. 51

The Narco-State is a social and political phenomenon that arises due to many factors, such as: a state of political anomia, the relationship between government authorities and drug trafficking, the involvement of people in the drug business in order to generate income; the development of a Narco-State is parallel with the development of the drug trafficking business, the activity fulfills the demand of drugs of the black market and for that it needs protection and organization.

One of the factors that influences a country to become a Narco-State is the denial, the denial of the authorities to accept drug trafficking as a social problem. The deterioration of the state begins with the bribery and corruption of government authorities and public institutions; a weak justice system allows drug traffickers to act with impunity, likewise, the Narco-State arises as soon as the gains of drug trafficking venture into the political life, creating networks of corruption in the state.

The post-Narco-State stage is a failed state, an unworkable state; The Narco-State can operate under a dictatorship and a democratic system of government, as it happened in 1980 in Bolivia during the Rule of Gral. Luis García Meza a dictatorship, or as is currently the case in Colombia and Mexico, states where drug trafficking has a lot of power in democracy; drug trafficking tends to work better in liberal, free-market and democratic societies, because of the government's less involvement, less harassing of the population, there is more freedom and therefore more opportunity to commit crimes.

The Narco-State evolves in a context of economic liberation at the international level, in a context of economic integration within the framework of globalization, where markets no longer have borders nor limits; it is in this environment that drug trafficking developed themselves to surpass the power of the state, turning the economic power they possess as a way to influence, in the highest spheres of political power.

Politics uses the Narco-State argument to take action against a state, the fact that a state is accused of being a Narco-State has serious and dangerous consequences, because this argument can be used politically to destroy different political figures, as it happened in 1989 when the President of Panama withdrew from power through military intervention, Manuel Noriega President of Panama was imprisoned in the United States for his relationship in drug trafficking;

Manuel Noriega, the President of Panama.

Source: https://www.taringa.net/+videos/invacion-a-panama-causa-justa-fotos-reales-y_i4ya2

The Narco-State argument is used for political purposes, as a political strategy; accusations of drug trafficking towards a government can create a political crisis and cause instability in a state, as was the case with the Government in Bolivia of General Luis García Meza, this administration was classified internationally as a Narco-State; the fight against drug trafficking becomes a political argument, a political weapon.

One of the negative consequences of being considered a Narco-State is that it stigmatizes the citizens of that state, all its citizens are considered to be drug traffickers, a stereotype is formed, it occurs with Colombians, Mexicans and Bolivians, the governments of these states are stigmatized and considered narco-governments, a scenario of constant violence is always in place, stable and permanent governance cannot be consolidated. In a narco-state the rights of individuals in society are threatened, likewise, the state becomes a sanctuary for drug traffickers and they can act with impunity, there is corruption in the institutions of the state, the money of drug trafficking corrupts public officials, police and military officials, and rulers do not have the moral authority to govern. The territory of a Narco-State becomes a conflictive zone, where the interests of many parties are involved, likewise, the authorities take advantage of the power they have to commit abuses, this results in a government that loses strength, legitimacy and stability.

Irregular armed groups arise groups that do not belong to the State, for example The self-defenses of Mexico, Los Pepe's (Persecuted by Pablo Escobar), MAS (Death to Kidnappers) of Colombia, etc. These armed groups, which in principle have political and ideological convictions, are engaged in committing kidnappings and in drug trafficking, as is the case of the FARC (Revolutionary Armed Forces of Colombia).

3.3.- Narco State and governance

The Governance in a Narco-State is not in force, because of the drug trafficking business that influences social and political structures; this company takes advantage of the absence of social cohesion, a clear sample of this is the existence of remote and abandoned areas, in which the authority of the Government is not in force and the drug trafficking business holds political power, delegitimizing and supplanting the State in different aspects, such as the meeting of social demands and the imposition of authority. *"The crisis of governance expresses the delegitimization of the State, when social demands are not met and are not resolved, ends in a dynamic in which the very essence of the rule of law is broken down"*.[26]

Likewise, history has proven that the use of drugs and the increase of addicts, are a threat to the status quo of society; drugs use changes

---

[26] ORTIZ JIMENEZ William, Mayo de 2006, pág. 67-68.

people's behavior and perception of reality, it changes their mind, establishing new ideologies and new social groups, as it happened with the hippie phenomenon in the United States in the 1960s.

Two hippies at the 1969 Woodstock Festival.

Source: https://www.english-online.at/history/1960s/society-and-change-in-the-sixties.htm

3.4.- Narco State and authority

Authority in a Narco-State has to do with the power that drug traffickers acquire in society, either because of its economic or political power; drug traffickers succeed in replacing the State in segments of society where government authority is weak, developing a kind of a parallel power, a parallel state, this happens in places where drug trafficking has a lot of power and influence. *"The rise of the narco as a "de facto" authority reveals that it is no exaggeration to start talking about a 'parallel narco state'">>.*[27]

3.5.- Narco State and organized crime

Organized crime refers to those criminal groups that have organization; According to Jorge Chabat, organized crime has the following characteristics:

"a.- It is not ideological and therefore has no political goals (the goal is profit). b.- It has a hierarchical structure. c.- Has a limited membership (often based on ethnic or kinship ties). d) It is an activity continued over time. e) Uses violence, or the threat of violence, and bribery. f) Displays a specific division of the work. g) It's a monopoly. h) It is governed by the explicit rules (including a secret code). To these classic characteristics, it should be added that: (i) It is a phenomenon that has become increasingly transnational. (j) Organized crime money often infiltrates legitimate economies and even has legitimate businesses and partners. k) Often the leadership is not involved in illicit activities. l) Uses violence in its relationship with other criminal organizations although

---

[27] CORONA CADENA Rubén I. 2009, p. 220.

there is sometimes cooperation. m) It usually penetrates the state to various extents".[28]

Fuente: http://www.lapiragua.co/nacional/contra-el-crimen-organizado/

Organized crime has as a characteristic the fact of having influence and political power, "*The power that these criminal gangs achieve is enormous and is precisely what allows them to assert themselves as "men of government", capable of imposing on society a how to proceed.*"[29] Organized crime in a Narco-State are those groups and organizations, which are engaged in carrying out different illicit activities in an organized and systematic way.

---

[28] CHABAT Jorge, septiembre 2005, pág. 2.
[29] CORONA CADENA, Rubén I, 2009, pág. 212.

Organized crime in Mexico, the division of the territory among the cartels in charge of the drug distribution.

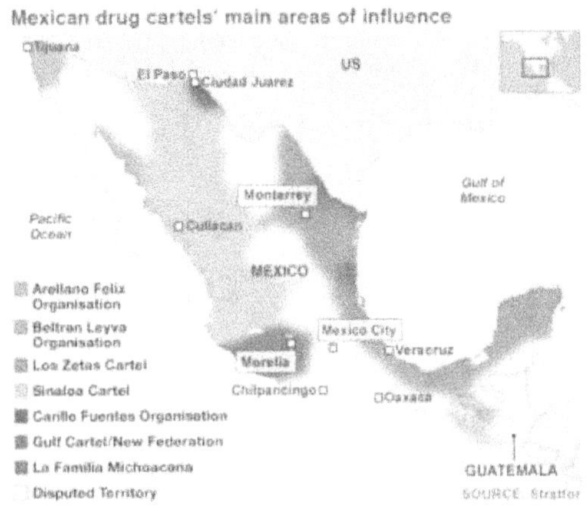

Source: https://www.bbc.com/mundo/america_latina/2010/09/10 0913_mexico_cartel_beltran_leyva_perfil_rg.shtml

3.6.- Narco State and corruption

Corruption refers to *"the action and effect of corrupting"*,[30] spoil something, to desicote, rot, pervert it, a murky and negative behavior; acts of corruption can be:

"The coimás, certain conduct of the holders of the public charges (bribery of officials, embezzlement of

---

[30] TERZANO BOUZON María Beatriz, p. 1.

property, trafficking of influences, abuse of functions, illegal enrichment...), bribery in the private sector, organized crime, money laundering, transfer of assets of illegal origin, etc.".[31]

In a Narco-State there is corruption in the institutions of the state, the government, the civil society is put at the mercy of the drug producers, likewise, the drug business acquires a degree of legitimacy. It is difficult to recognize that a state is a narco-state, there must be acts of violence, an internal war, a power struggle between drug traffickers and the government, there must be allegations of drug trafficking against political leaders. A state can be regarded as a Narco-State, when the drug trafficking business becomes a problem and affects the security of the State, the fight against it becomes state policy.

---

[31] Ídem.

Source: https://www.celag.org/a-quien-conviene-corrupcion-america-latina/

Therefore the corruption in this writing is the perversion of the government authorities, it is the negative conduct on the part of public officials, it is the corruption of the state.

3.7.- On the concept of drugs

According to the Psych pedagogical Cabinet of the University of Granada, *"A drug is a substance that alters the normal functioning of the body once it comes into contact with it. Examples of drugs include alcohol, nicotine, caffeine, inhalants, steroids, marijuana and cocaine"*.[32] Drugs are very addictive and can create dependence.

---

[32] GABINETE PSICOPEDAGOGICO, 2001, pág. 1.

Likewise, the WHO (World Health Organization) defines drugs as:

"Any substance that, introduced into the body by any route of administration, results in an alteration in some way, of the natural functioning of the central nervous system of the individual and is also capable of creating dependence, whether psychological, physical or both".[33]

Source: https://www.mas.org.ar/?p=8817

For the United Nations Office on Drugs and Crime (UNODC) in Bolivia, the term drug is:

"...it refers to substances that is subject to international control. In medicine it refers to any substance capable of preventing or curing diseases or improving physical or mental well-being. In pharmacology the term drug refers to any chemical

---

[33] HORMILOUGE Marcela Cristina, 1997, pág. 1.

agent that alters the biochemical physiological processes of tissues and organisms. In the common use, the term drug often refers to psychoactive drugs and often illicit drugs".[34]

Source:
http://uraldaily.ru/proisshestviya/oktyabr/02/ugolovnoe-delo-organizatora-i-uchastnikov-narkokartelya-napravleno-v-sud

[34] MINISTERIO DE GOBIERNO, ESTADO PLURINACIONAL DE BOLIVIA, 2015, Pág. 27

CONCLUSIONS

1.- The main and common feature in all the States considered Narco-States is a socio-political context in which the drug trafficking business has become relevant; there is no willingness or capacity on the part of the Government to fight the trafficking and production of drugs, because of the corruption of the authorities, it is in this social scenario that a Narco-State is established.

2.- It can be said that a Full Narco-State fails to establish itself as long as there is a segment of society, which regards this industry as immoral and unacceptable; it is also sufficient to exist a social scenario of symbiosis between the State and the drug business for a country to be considered a Narco-State, this relationship of interdependence can be one of antagonism or of a peaceful nature; likewise, it is not imperative that the drug trafficking has to take over the whole country, it is sufficient for the drug business to acquire importance in the social and political context of the State.

3.- The concept of Narco-State is used to describe a state in which the drug trafficking industry has been established with a high degree of political, economic and cultural power. There is a symbiosis between what is the state and the drug trafficking business; a social scenario is in place where this industry has the capacity to challenge the authority of the state, there is corruption and the drug production and trafficking is common.

Example of a Narco-State:

During the Government of the Gral. Luis García Meza in Bolivia (1980-1981) there was in force a scenario of political anomie that led to the establishment of a Narco-State. The crisis of political anomie manifested itself in this historical period and is one of the theoretical arguments and sustenance's, for the characterization of the Bolivian state as a Narco-State during that period. It can be said that Bolivia was a Narco-State in that period, for the validity of the factors that make it.

Likewise, the country of Panama was also considered a Narco-state during the administration of Manuel Noriega.

BIBLIOGRAPHY

ALMADA Marcos, 07 / 2005, Narcoculture: music, marijuana and lots of action, The culture of drug trafficking in the entertainment media, , dialogues, proposals, stories for a World Citizenship, obtained from : http://base.d-p-h.info/es/fiches/dph/fiche-dph-7137.html

ARISTIZABAL VILLADA John Jairo, 2006, *PLAN COLOMBIA AND ANTIDROGA POLICY OF THE UNITED STATES*, undergraduate work to opt for the degree of sociologist, Faculty of Social and Human Sciences, Department of Sociology, University of Antioquia, Medellin-Colombia. Obtained from http://bibliotecadigital.udea.edu.co/dspace/bitstream/10495/250/1/PlanColombiaPoliticaAntidrogas.pdf"

CHABAT Jorge, September 2005, *Narcotragy and State: The Discreet Charm of Corruption*, Published in Free Letters. Obtained from http://www2.congreso.gob.pe/sicr/cendocbib/con4_uibd.nsf/3B5233D86839795405257DFE006F9329/$FILE/Narcotr%C3%A1fico_y_Estado-El_discreto_encanto_de_la_corrupci%C3%B3n.pdf"

CONTRERAS VELASCO Oscar, *The evolution of drug trafficking in Mexico.* Obtained from www-lanic.lib.utexas.edu/Project/etext/llilas/ilassa/2010/Velasco.pdf

CORONA CADENA Rubén I. 2009, *The Narco, Parallel State*, ITESO Publications (Instituto Tecnológico y de Estudios Superiores de Occidente), Revista Analysis Plural 2o Semestre 2008, Jalisco-Mexico. Obtained from:
"https://rei.iteso.mx/bitstream/handle/11117/813/AP%202008-2%20SEM%2013_El%20narco.pdf?sequence=2"

PSICOPEDAGOGIC GABINETE, 2001, *Substance Use and Abuse*, University of Granada. Obtained from http://www.ugr.es/~ve/pdf/consumo.pdf

HOBBES Thomas, *Leviathan,* Politician's Library. Obtained from http://www.uruguaypiensa.org.uy/imgnoticias/749.pdf

HORMILOUGE Marcela Cristina, 1997, *Drug Misuse Theme.* Obtained from www.oocities.org/marcelah_arg/qdroga.pdf

MAQUIAVELO Nicholas, 1999, *Prince,* Edited by elaleph.com, ©1999 – Copyright www.elaleph.com. Obtenido de https://mega.nz/#!PYcTABxa!rnXqmWAGWMw6S CYlKUGLESRFuxB5lAxXJofH6g34nWY

MINISTRY OF GOVERNMENT, PLURINATIONAL STATE OF BOLIVIA, 2015, DRUG PROBLEMS, BOLIVIA. Obtained from https://www.unodc.org/documents/bolivia/Prev_Problematica_de_las_drogas.pdf

UNITED NATIONS, October 2008, *THE THREAT OF NARCOTTRAFICO IN AMERICA, Office against Drugs and Crime.* Obtained from https://www.unodc.org/documents/data-and-analysis/Studies/Reporte_OEA_2008.pdf

NAVARRETE FRIAS Carolina y THOUMI Francisco E, 2005, *Illegal drugs and human rights of peasants and indigenous communities: the case of Bolivia*, Printed by the United Nations Educational, Scientific and Cultural Organization. ©UNESCO, Paris – France. Obtained from http://digitallibrary.unesco.org/shs/most/gsdl/collect/most/index/assoc/HASHbb37.dir/doc.pdf

ORTIZ JIMENEZ William, May 2006, *THE PARAESTADOS IN COLOMBIA*, DOCTORAL THESIS PRESENTATED AS A REQUIREMENT TO OPT FOR THE TITLE OF DOCTOR IN SOCIOLOGY, Editorial of the University of Granada, Faculty of Sociology and Political Sciences, UNIVERSITY OF GRANADA, Granada-Spain. Obtained from https://hera.ugr.es/tesisugr/16183605.pdf

OVALLE MARROQUIN Lilian Paola, Marzo 2010, *Drug trafficking and power. Field of struggle for legitimacy*, Universidad Autónoma de Baja California. Obtained from atheneadigital.net/article/download/n17-ovalle/632-pdf-es

PALACIOS Marco y SERRANO Monica, *COLOMBIA AND MEXICO DRUG TRAFFICKING VIOLENCE.* Obtained from https://cei.colmex.mx/Estudios%20sobre%20violenc ia/Estudios%20Violencia%20M%C3%A9xico%20Ma teriales%20recibidos/Grandes%20problemas/Cap%C 3%ADtulo%204%20(Serrano%20y%20Palacios).pdf

PEREZ ROJAS Cesar Kenny, 2018, *Political Anomie and Narco-State in Bolivia. Government of the Gral. Luis García Meza (July 17, 1980 – August 4, 1981),* research work produced by the university Cesar Kenny Pérez Rojas, to obtain the academic degree of bachelor's degree in political science, political science career, UMSS, Cochabamba – Bolivia.

ROUSSEAU Juan Jacob, 1999, *THE SOCIAL CONTRACT OR PRINCIPLES OF POLITICAL RIGHT,* Edited by elaleph.com, ©1999 – Copyright elaleph.com. Obtained from http://www.enxarxa.com/biblioteca/ROUSSEAU%2 0El%20Contrato%20Social.pdf

RUIZ DIAZ Roberto Labrano, *THE STATE OF RIGHT OF SOME ELEMENTS AND CONDITIONS FOR ITS EFFECTIVE EFFECTIVENESS, Obtained from* http://www.tprmercosur.org/es/docum/biblio/Ruiz _Diaz_Labrano_El_Estado_de_Derecho.pdf

SOBERON Ricardo, (18-7-2018), *Narcopolitics and its effects on widespread corruption in the Peruvian State*, News. Pe. Obtained from http://www.noticiasser.pe/index.php/opinion/la-narcopolitica-y-sus efectos-en-la-corrupción-generalizada-en-el-estado-peruano

TERZANO BOUZON María Beatriz, *CORRUPTION: CONCEPT, REALITY AND REFELEXIONS.* Obtained from http://www.uca.edu.ar/uca/common/grupo3/vc/file s/segunda%20parte/03-Terzano.pdf

VICEPRESIDENCE OF SUPERVISION OF PREVENTIVE PROCESSES, CNBV, Obtained from:https://www.cnbv.gob.mx/CNBV/Documents /VSPP_Lavado%20de%20Dinero.pdf

WEBER Max, *THE POLITICIAN AND THE SCIENTIST,* Document prepared by the Computer and Productive Networks Program of the General San Martin National University (UNSAM). Obtained from: http://www.hacer.org/pdf/WEBER.pdf

INTERNET

https://ssociologos.com/2019/03/03/el-peru-es-un-narcoestado/

https://mundo.sputniknews.com/seguridad/201804161077935653-europa-madrid-paris-trafico-drogas-seguridad/

http://www.lapiragua.co/nacional/contra-el-crimen-organizado/

https://www.celag.org/a-quien-conviene-corrupcion-america-latina/

https://www.mas.org.ar/?p=8817

https://www.excelsior.com.mx/expresiones/2015/05/05/1022534

https://www.infobae.com/america/colombia/2019/11/24/a-30-anos-del-dia-que-pablo-escobar-hizo-explotar-un-avion-comercial-y-mato-a-110-personas-pero-se-salvo-la-unica-a-la-que-queria-asesinar/

https://www.dineroenimagen.com/economia/como-funciona-el-lavado-de-dinero/87011

https://www.amazon.ca/Pablo-Escobar-Patron-Del-Part/dp/B00BZC00Z2

https://www.taringa.net/+videos/invacion-a-panama-causa-justa-fotos-reales-y_i4ya2

https://www.bbc.com/mundo/america_latina/2010/09/100913_mexico_cartel_beltran_leyva_perfil_rg.shtml

This edition was finished
printing on January 1, 2020
in the CK workshops
Cochabamba, Bolivia.